SCHOOL STRUGGLES

A 4-week course to help Christian teenagers study more effectively, improve grades, resist cheating and balance their active schedules

by Linda Snyder

School Struggles

First Printing

Credits
Edited by Stephen Parolini
Cover designed by Jill Bendykowski and DeWain Stoll
Interior designed by Judy Atwood Bienick and Jan Aufdemberge
Cover photo by David Priest and Brenda Rundback
Photos on pp. 17, 25 and 32 by David Priest

ISBN 1-55945-201-3
Printed in the United States of America

CONTENTS

INTRODUCTION

SCHOOL STRUGGLES

Ticktock, ticktock, ticktock. Every eye is glued to the clock. Three minutes. Two minutes. One minute to go.

The bell rings. Then—mayhem! Teenagers rush into the halls, unfazed by the stampedelike congestion. Locker doors swing open, then slam shut. Teenagers pour out of the building as if it were on fire.

School's out.

According to a survey from Seventeen magazine:

- Nearly nine out of 10 kids today feel they're under a lot of pressure to get good grades.
- Six out of 10 young people say education is one of the three most critical problems in America today.

- One out of four teenagers would cheat on an important exam if they could be sure they wouldn't get caught.

School is the number one stressor for adolescents. Because of the tremendous emphasis placed on academic success, even the smallest failure in school can seem huge to teenagers.

Many students see high school as the barometer of their future success. Grades, athletics, activities and interpersonal relationships gain a new significance in high school as college, career and social futures begin taking recognizable shape.

Suicide, debilitating physical conditions, grade paranoia and burnout can all be caused by school stress. Though we can't remove all the stressors, we can help teenagers cope.

This 4-week course will help your teenagers deal with school stress. They'll view success from a biblical perspective. They'll see how Jesus touched the life of a cheater. They'll discover the importance of building a solid foundation at school. And they'll learn how to deal with worry and burnout.

HOW TO USE THIS COURSE

ACTIVE LEARNING

Think back on an important lesson you've learned. Did you learn it from reading about it? from hearing about it? from something you experienced? Chances are, the most important lessons you've learned came from something you experienced. That's what active learning is—learning by doing. And active learning is a key element in Group's Active Bible Curriculum.

Active learning leads students in doing things that help them understand important principles, messages and ideas. It's a discovery process that helps kids internalize what they learn.

Each lesson section in Group's Active Bible Curriculum plays an important part in active learning.

The **Opener** involves kids in the topic in fun and unusual ways.

The **Action and Reflection** includes an experience designed to evoke specific feelings in the students. This section also processes those feelings through "How did you feel?" questions and applies the message to situations kids face.

The **Bible Application** actively connects the topic with the Bible. It helps kids see how the Bible is relevant to the situations they face.

The **Commitment** helps students internalize the Bible's message and commit to make changes in their lives.

The **Closing** funnels the lesson's message into a time of creative reflection and prayer.

When you put all the sections together, you get a lesson that's fun to teach—and kids get messages they'll remember.

BEFORE THE 4-WEEK SESSION

- Read the Introduction, the Course Objectives and This Course at a Glance (p. 8).
- Decide how you'll publicize the course using the art on the Publicity Page (p. 9). Prepare fliers, newsletter articles and posters as needed.
- Look at the Bonus Ideas (p. 43) and decide which ones you'll use.

BEFORE EACH LESSON

● Read the opening statements, Objectives and Bible Basis for the lesson. The Bible Basis shows how specific passages relate to senior highers today.

● Choose which Opener and Closing options to use. Each is appropriate for a different kind of group. The first option is often more active than the second.

● Gather necessary supplies from This Lesson at a Glance.

● Read each section of the lesson. Adjust where necessary for your class size and meeting room.

HELPFUL HINTS

● The approximate minutes listed give you an idea of how long each activity will take. Each lesson is designed to take 35 to 60 minutes. Shorten or lengthen activities as needed to fit your group.

● If you see you're going to have extra time, do an activity or two from the "If You Still Have Time . . . " box or from the Bonus Ideas (p. 43.)

● Dive into the activities with the kids. Don't be a spectator. The lesson will be more successful and rewarding to both you and your students.

● The answers given after discussion questions are responses your students *might* give. They aren't the only answers or the "right" answers. If needed, use them to spark discussion. Kids won't always say what you wish they'd say. That's why some of the responses given are negative or controversial. If someone responds negatively, don't be shocked. Accept the person, and use the opportunity to explore other angles of the issue.

COURSE OBJECTIVES

By the end of this course your students will:

- define success from a Christian perspective;
- study how specific Bible passages can help them deal with failure, cheating and other school stresses;
- identify the negative impact of cheating and learn to deal with the temptation to cheat;
- assess their study habits and attitudes;
- examine their academic and non-academic priorities; and
- learn to set goals and reach them one step at a time.

THIS COURSE AT A GLANCE

Before you dive into the lessons, familiarize yourself with each lesson aim. Then read the scripture passages.

- Study them as a background to the lessons.
- Use them as a basis for your personal devotions.
- Think about how they relate to kids' circumstances today.

LESSON 1: REPORT CARD BLUES

Lesson Aim: To help teenagers put grades into a positive perspective.

Bible Basis: Romans 12:4-8; Luke 15:11-32; and Proverbs 9:9-12.

LESSON 2: THE CONSEQUENCES OF CHEATING

Lesson Aim: To help teenagers understand the negative results of cheating and how to avoid the temptation to cheat.

Bible Basis: Leviticus 19:11; Exodus 20:15; and Luke 19:1-10.

LESSON 3: I DON'T HAVE TIME FOR HOMEWORK

Lesson Aim: To help teenagers recognize the value of studying.

Bible Basis: Matthew 7:24-27 and Matthew 25:14-29.

LESSON 4: SO MUCH TO DO . . .

Lesson Aim: To help teenagers manage their time, balancing activities and academics.

Bible Basis: Ecclesiastes 3:1-8 and Luke 10:38-42.

PUBLICITY PAGE

Grab your senior highers' attention! Copy this page, then cut and paste the art of your choice in your church bulletin or newsletter to advertise this course on school struggles. Or copy and use the ready-made flier as a bulletin insert.

Splash this art on posters, fliers or even post-cards! Just add the vital details: the date and time the course begins, and where you'll meet.

It's that simple.

SCHOOL STRUGGLES

SCHOOL STRUGGLES

School Struggles

A 4-week senior high course on grades, cheating, homework and managing your time

Come to ______________________________

On ______________________________

At ______________________________

Come learn how your faith can help you beat school stress!

REPORT CARD BLUES

LESSON 1

Grades are the most nerve-racking part of school for kids today. Low grades and low self-esteem often go hand in hand. And competition runs high for the top grade honors. When grades get out of perspective, report cards become marks of failure or success rather than points of progress.

LESSON AIM

To help teenagers put grades into a positive perspective.

OBJECTIVES

Students will:

- **examine school tensions;**
- **discuss how God sees success;**
- **explore what the Bible teaches about failure and success; and**
- **evaluate their progress according to God's measure of success.**

BIBLE BASIS

ROMANS 12:4-8
LUKE 15:11-32
PROVERBS 9:9-12

Look up the following scriptures. Then read the background paragraphs to see how the passages relate to your senior highers.

In **Romans 12:4-8**, Paul teaches that we are members of one body, yet each has a different gift.

Paul's message to the church in Rome included this warning against false pride. His description of the church as one body with many different members was intended to help the readers accept their specific—yet differing—gifts as Christians.

Society's view of success is narrow. Paul's description of these seven gifts broadens that view to include many kinds of success. From this, teenagers can learn that getting straight A's isn't the only measure of success.

In **Luke 15:11-32**, Jesus tells the parable of the prodigal son.

In this parable, the prodigal son was a failure. Pig slop was proof of his failing grade. Still, the father accepted his son with unconditional love.

High school kids often feel like the son who failed his father. This passage can reassure them that God loves them regardless of their grade-point average.

In **Proverbs 9:9-12**, Solomon explains the way of wisdom.

Solomon's definition of wisdom differs greatly from the definition in today's school systems. According to Solomon, wisdom begins with the fear of God and leads to knowledge of him. Solomon also says that a wise person will continue to seek wisdom.

Teenagers can learn two lessons from this passage. They can learn that God's definition of wisdom isn't based on their school grades, but seeking wisdom is a good endeavor.

THIS LESSON AT A GLANCE

Section	Minutes	What Students Will Do	Supplies
Opener (Option 1)	5 to 10	**Tension Targets**—List top school tensions.	Newsprint, markers, tape, rubber bands
(Option 2)		**Report Card Day**—Role-play parents and teenagers discussing grades.	
Action and Reflection	10 to 15	**Foiled Again**—Create aluminum foil reflections of failure.	Aluminum foil, markers, newsprint, tape
Bible Application	10 to 15	**Wisdom**—Discover what the Bible says about failure.	Bibles, newsprint, markers
Commitment	5 to 10	**Yearbook Hall of Fame**—Complete a handout of "gifts" and yearbook profiles.	"Yearbook Hall of Fame" handouts (p. 17), pencils
Closing (Option 1)	5 to 10	**Success Symbols**—Create school success symbols from a Christian perspective.	Foil, Bibles
(Option 2)		**God's Report Card**—Set a goal for improving grades on a "spiritual" report card.	Spiritual Report Card from Foiled Again

The Lesson

OPTION 1: TENSION TARGETS

Ask:

- **How important is it to get good grades? Explain.** (Very important, they affect my career options; not very important, nobody cares except teachers and parents.)

Form groups of no more than five. Hand out newsprint and markers to each group. Have groups each draw a large circle in the middle of their newsprint and quickly list in the circle all the school-related pressures teenagers feel. After a minute, call time. Have groups share their lists with each other.

Say: **You've just expressed some of the negative aspects of school. The pressure to get good grades creates tension and stress. Now, think of some "tension breakers"—ways to put school and grades in perspective. List these on the newsprint outside your circle of tensions.**

After two minutes, have groups each tape their newsprint to the wall. For each tension breaker listed by a group, give that group a rubber band. Then have volunteers from each group shoot the group's rubber bands at the circle of tensions. The team with the most hits inside their circle gets an A for the activity.

Say: **School can be stressful. And grades are a major stress factor because we often measure our success by the grades we get. Today we'll compare school grades with how God measures success.**

OPTION 2: REPORT CARD DAY

Ask for two volunteers. Have them leave the room while you explain the next activity.

Form two groups. Tell teenagers they'll be playing the role of the volunteers' parents on report card day. Tell the first group to praise the A-student for a job well-done and berate the D-student for being so stupid. Tell them to be vicious in their attack on the D-student. Have the second group praise the A-student and calmly discuss ways to help the D-student raise his or her grades.

Invite the volunteers back into the room. Explain to them that today is report card day. Then tell one volunteer he or she got straight A's and the other he or she got mostly D's. Be careful not to stereotype the students you choose for these roles. It's best to choose volunteers who you know are good students. Have them stand in front of the first group. Say to the volunteers: **Imagine this group is your parents. Tell them your grades, then respond to their comments.**

After a minute or so, stop the role play and have the

OPENER

(5 to 10 minutes)

volunteers stand in front of the second group. Say to the volunteers: **Once again, imagine this group is your parents. Tell them your grades and respond to their comments.**

After another minute or so, stop the role play.

Ask:

- **What was the difference between the two role plays?** (The parents' reactions; the students' attitudes.)
- **Which of the parent groups was the best motivator? Explain.** (The first group, they scared the kid into doing better next time; the second group, they were calm and discussed ways to improve things.)

Say: **Grades are a touchy subject in many homes. Many parents and teenagers measure success by the number of A's on a report card. Today we'll look at how God sees success and compare that to our view of grades and school.**

ACTION AND REFLECTION

(10 to 15 minutes)

FOILED AGAIN

Give a 10- or 12-inch square of aluminum foil to each person. Have kids each look at their reflection in the foil. Say: **I'll read a list of school and grade stresses. Each time you hear one that makes you feel stressed, crumple your aluminum foil a little.**

Read the following words and phrases:

Midterms	Parental pressures
Finals	Classes you don't like
Pop quizzes	Homework
Essay questions	Multiple choice questions
Teachers	Low grades

Say: **Open up the crumpled foil and look at your reflection again. When we feel pressured to succeed in school, it crumples the way we see ourselves. Look at your reflection in the aluminum foil. Has your self-esteem been wrinkled by school pressures? Try to restore the foil to its original state.**

Pause while students try this.

Say: **We can't do it can we? But God can restore our self-esteem when we've been wrinkled by the pressures to succeed.**

Form a circle. Read aloud Romans 12:4-8. Have teenagers list subject areas from this passage that God might put on a spiritual report card. Write these on a sheet of newsprint and tape it to the wall. Then ask students to list subjects that are on their school report cards. Write these on another sheet of newsprint and tape it beside the first one.

Ask:

- **What are the differences between the two report cards?** (The school one focuses on academics and the spiritual one focuses on attitudes and behavior.)
- **On which report card would you rather be graded? Explain.** (The school report card, it's only one part of your

life; the spiritual report card, it's the only one that matters.)

● **On which report card would it be hardest to get straight A's? Explain.** (The school report card, I'm not too good at school; the spiritual report card, only Jesus is perfect in all these areas.)

● **Which report card best measures your success? Explain.** (The spiritual one, doing God's will is being successful; the school one, good grades mean higher salaries.)

● **If God's measure of success is more important, does that mean school isn't important? Why or why not?** (No, school is important because God wants us to do our best; yes, school isn't important because God has bigger plans for us.)

BIBLE APPLICATION

(10 to 15 minutes)

WISDOM

Say: **Though the Bible doesn't mention report cards or grades directly, Jesus does tell a story about someone who failed.**

Form two groups. Have each read Luke 15:11-32 and briefly discuss what it says about failure.

Ask:

● **How can the son's failures be compared to failure in school?** (I feel like the prodigal son when I do poorly on a test; it's hard to admit when I make poor choices.)

● **What does Jesus say about failure?** (No failure is too big to be forgiven; failure is painful; failure may result from inappropriate actions.)

● **Can failure be reversed? Explain.** (Yes, you usually have a second chance; no, you can't erase the consequences.)

● **What can we learn about success in school from this scripture?** (Good grades don't come without hard work; it's never too late to change your ways and do better in school; God loves me no matter what my grade-point average is.)

Form a circle. Then write the word "wisdom" on a sheet of newsprint, and ask students to define the word. List their definitions on the newsprint. Then have someone read aloud Proverbs 9:9-12. Have teenagers define wisdom based on this passage. Then discuss the similarities and differences in the definitions.

COMMITMENT

(5 to 10 minutes)

YEARBOOK HALL OF FAME

Ask:

● **At the end of your senior year, what will your yearbook say about you? What measure of success will you have attained according to God's report card? the school's report card?**

Give students each a copy of the "Yearbook Hall of Fame" handout (p. 17) and a pencil. Encourage teenagers to be honest and realistic as they complete the form.

When teenagers are finished, form pairs. Have partners

talk about their completed handouts. Tell them they don't have to discuss answers they feel uncomfortable sharing.

Then have teenagers each choose one or two "Senior Stats" that describe their partner's strengths. Have them tell each other why they appreciate those qualities in their partner.

CLOSING
(5 to 10 minutes)

OPTION 1: SUCCESS SYMBOLS

Form groups of no more than four. Give groups each several sheets of used aluminum foil. Say: **Use the foil to create a school success symbol. The symbol should illustrate how you view success from a Christian perspective.**

Have groups complete their foil creations and present them to the rest of the class. Form a circle and say: **It's important to be the best student you can be. But school grades aren't the only indicators of success. We must also develop our God-given talents and abilities.**

Place the foil creations in the center of the circle. Read Romans 12:2 and close with prayer.

OPTION 2: GOD'S REPORT CARD

Have students look at the spiritual report card they helped create in the Foiled Again activity. Say: **Silently find your "best subject" on this report card.**

Pause. Say: **Now look for an area where you can improve. Think about specific things you can do to improve your grade in this area.**

Close by having students pray silently to do their best in God's eyes and at school.

If You Still Have Time ...

The Great Debate—Form two teams. Assign one team the argument: Report cards should be pass/fail. Assign the other team the argument: Report cards should be graded A through F.

Give the teams five minutes to brainstorm supporting arguments for their positions. Then have a debate by allowing each side to present its arguments—one at a time.

You Be The Judge—Call out the following references one at a time. Have volunteers take turns reading them. After each scripture is read, ask the teenagers to grade the Bible character. Tell students the grade they give must be agreed upon unanimously.

- Genesis 17:17-19 (Abraham)
- Genesis 27:5-26 (Jacob)
- Exodus 2:11-14 (Moses)
- Jonah 1:1-3 (Jonah)
- Luke 4:1-13 (Jesus)
- Luke 22:54-62 (Peter)

Discuss the differences in the grades.

Ask:

- **Can anyone be perfect? Explain.**
- **What does this tell us about our anxiety about grades?**
- **If we know we won't ever be perfect, does that mean we should stop trying? Why or why not?**

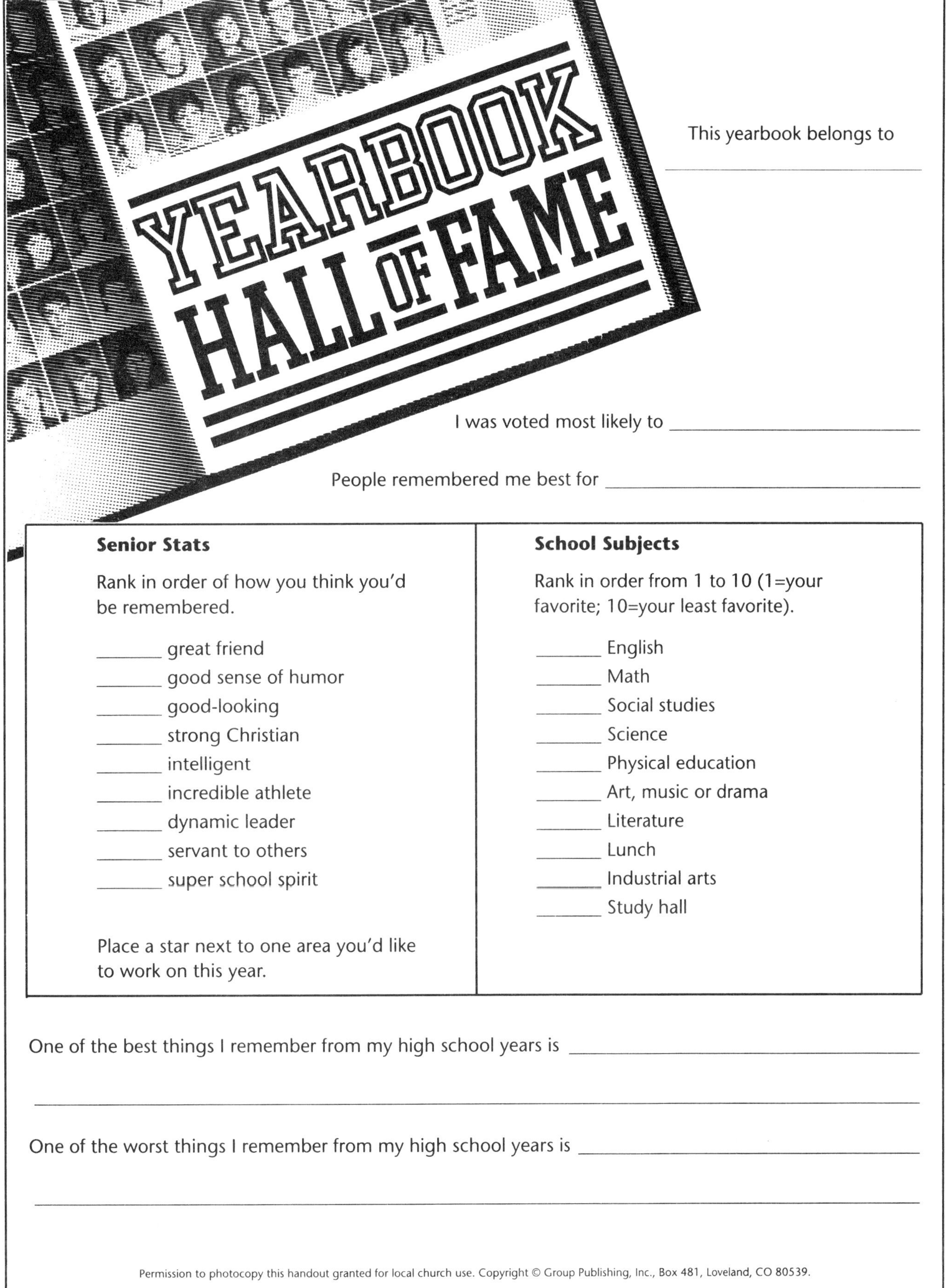

This yearbook belongs to ____________________

I was voted most likely to ____________________

People remembered me best for ____________________

Senior Stats

Rank in order of how you think you'd be remembered.

_______ great friend
_______ good sense of humor
_______ good-looking
_______ strong Christian
_______ intelligent
_______ incredible athlete
_______ dynamic leader
_______ servant to others
_______ super school spirit

Place a star next to one area you'd like to work on this year.

School Subjects

Rank in order from 1 to 10 (1=your favorite; 10=your least favorite).

_______ English
_______ Math
_______ Social studies
_______ Science
_______ Physical education
_______ Art, music or drama
_______ Literature
_______ Lunch
_______ Industrial arts
_______ Study hall

One of the best things I remember from my high school years is ____________________

____

One of the worst things I remember from my high school years is ____________________

____

LESSON 2

THE CONSEQUENCES OF CHEATING

"Doesn't everybody cheat?"
"What's the big deal about cheating?"
"Why shouldn't I cheat?"

When it comes to cheating, these are the questions teenagers ask. But what they should ask is: "Who's really being cheated?"

LESSON AIM

To help teenagers understand the negative results of cheating and how to avoid the temptation to cheat.

OBJECTIVES

Students will:

- **discuss common cheating temptations;**
- **explore what the Bible teaches about cheating;**
- **brainstorm ways to avoid cheating; and**
- **commit to avoid the temptation to cheat.**

BIBLE BASIS

EXODUS 20:15
LEVITICUS 19:11
LUKE 19:1-10

Look up the following scriptures. Then read the background paragraphs to see how the passages relate to your senior highers.

Both **Exodus 20:15** and **Leviticus 19:11** state don't steal, lie or deal falsely with one another.

Old Testament law was black and white on the issue of stealing or cheating. The laws outlined in Exodus and Leviticus stated that all cheating or lying was wrong.

The Old Testament message is still valid for teenagers today. Cheating on a little pop quiz might not seem like much, but according to scripture, it's just as bad as cheating on a college entrance exam.

In **Luke 19:1-10**, Zacchaeus chooses to follow Jesus and repay those he cheated.

Tax collectors were despised in Jesus' day. They were well-known for their cheating and unlawful dealings. So Zacchaeus' dramatic change caused quite a commotion among those close to Jesus.

Teenagers can learn a lot from Zacchaeus' story. Cheating was a way of life for Zacchaeus, just as it is for some teenagers. But just as Zacchaeus was able to change his lifestyle, Jesus can help teenagers learn not to cheat.

THIS LESSON AT A GLANCE

Section	Minutes	What Students Will Do	Supplies
Opener (Option 1)	5 to 10	**Bible Pop Quiz**—Complete a pop quiz and respond to a student who cheats.	"Bible Pop Quiz" handouts (p. 24), pencils, prize
(Option 2)		**Gruesome Twosomes**—Identify cheating temptations.	Paper, pencils
Action and Reflection	15 to 20	**Here Comes the Judge**—Participate in trials for cheating incidents.	"Case Studies" handouts (p. 25), Bibles
Bible Application	10 to 15	**Up a Tree**—Rewrite Zacchaeus' story as a school-related story.	Bibles, paper, pencils
Commitment	5 to 10	**Students Against Cheating**—Create "anti-cheating" posters.	Posterboard, markers
Closing (Option 1)	up to 5	**Cheating Scars**—Examine the negative implications of cheating.	Black construction paper, pencils, erasers
(Option 2)		**Anti-Cheaters Club**—Affirm a commitment against cheating.	Posters from Students Against Cheating, markers

The Lesson

OPENER
(5 to 10 minutes)

OPTION 1: BIBLE POP QUIZ

Before class, ask a student to help you with the opening activity. Explain to the volunteer that everyone will take the same quiz, but that he or she will get a quiz with the correct answers already marked. Mark one copy of the quiz with the correct answers. Then have the volunteer pretend to complete the quiz while everyone else does.

Say: **Today we have a pop quiz to start the lesson. You'll have two minutes to complete the quiz as best as you can. The person with the highest score will win a prize.**

Have teenagers sit in separate areas of the room. Give each person a copy of the "Bible Pop Quiz" (p. 24) and a pencil. Be sure to give your volunteer the marked copy. After two minutes, call time and have students exchange papers for grading. Go over the answers and have teenagers grade the papers. Determine the winner and award the prize. A food prize works best.

The answers are: 1. too young (Jeremiah 1:6); 2. Bathsheba (2 Samuel 11); 3. Ezekiel (Ezekiel 1:10); 4. Silas, Philippi (Acts 16:25-27); Hosea, Gomer (Hosea 1:2); 6. Baalam (Numbers 22:28); 7. Seth, Abel (Genesis 4).

Ask:

- **How did you feel when you were given the pop quiz?** (Angry; stupid; confident.)
- **Were you tempted to cheat? Why or why not?** (No, I don't cheat; no, this wasn't an important test; yes, I wanted the prize.)

Tell the students about the paper with the pre-written answers.

Then ask:

- **How do you feel knowing that the person who won the prize cheated?** (Angry; upset; it doesn't bother me.)
- **Was it fair for the "cheater" to win the prize? Why or why not?** (No, he or she didn't have to struggle with the answers like we did; no, he or she didn't deserve it.)
- **Who gets cheated when someone cheats?** (The cheater; the other students; the teacher.)

OPTION 2: GRUESOME TWOSOMES

Form pairs. Give each pair a piece of paper and a pencil.

Say: **When is cheating appropriate? With your partner, list any times you think cheating might be okay in school.**

After partners finish their lists, have them each read them aloud. Then discuss briefly the positive and negative consequences of cheating in school.

Ask:

- **Who gets cheated when someone cheats? Explain.** (The cheater, he or she doesn't learn anything; the others in the class, their grades are lowered; the teacher, he or she is fooled.)

HERE COMES THE JUDGE

ACTION AND REFLECTION
(15 to 20 minutes)

Form groups of three, five or seven. If necessary, join a group so each group has an odd number of participants. Give groups each a copy of the "Case Studies" handout (p. 25). Tell groups they'll have 90 seconds for each case study. Say: **As a group, you must discuss the case and determine the proper punishment. In order for a punishment to be approved, a majority of the group members must agree on it.**

Have groups spend 90 seconds on each of the four cases. Then form a circle and have groups share their punishments with the other groups.

Ask:

- **How did the punishments in the various studies compare?** (Some were more severe; they were all about the same.)
- **Is it right for the punishment to be tougher in one case than another? Explain.** (No, all cheating is bad; yes, cheating to get into college is worse than cheating on a pop quiz.)
- **How is cheating like stealing?** (You're taking something that doesn't belong to you.)

Have someone read aloud Exodus 20:15 and Leviticus 19:11. Say: **The Bible doesn't differentiate between big lies and little lies, or between stealing something little or stealing something big. It says all stealing and all lying—and therefore all cheating—are wrong. Do you agree? Why or why not?** (Yes, cheating only hurts you—it can't help; no, sometimes it's okay to cheat—when you don't hurt anyone else.)

UP A TREE

BIBLE APPLICATION
(10 to 15 minutes)

Form groups of no more than six, and give groups each a Bible, paper and a pencil. Have groups each read Luke 19:1-10 and rewrite the story, updating it to a modern, school setting where Zacchaeus is a student who cheats. Ask them to include reactions the crowd had to Jesus befriending Zacchaeus. Then have groups each prepare a one-minute skit based on their new story.

Have groups present their skits.

Then ask:

- **How are you like Zacchaeus?** (I'm not always honest; I'm not like him; I want to be better.)
- **By his actions and words, what does Jesus say about cheaters?** (Cheaters are people too; nobody's perfect; cheaters can change their ways.)
- **How can people overcome the temptation to cheat?** (By obeying God's law; by avoiding situations where cheating is possible; by studying harder.)

COMMITMENT
(5 to 10 minutes)

STUDENTS AGAINST CHEATING

Say: **It's easy to talk about not cheating. But it's not always easy to resist cheating when school is competitive and grades are important.**

Form groups of three or four. Give each group posterboard and markers. Have them each design a poster promoting the attitude that cheating is wrong.

After groups complete their posters, tape the posters to the wall. Allow students a minute or so to look at the other groups' posters. As they look at the posters, have them each silently commit to working on avoiding the temptation to cheat in one specific area of their lives.

Thank each teenager for his or her commitment. Have teenagers walk around and encourage each other not to cheat. Suggest students shake hands, pat each other on the back and say, "You don't have to cheat because you're a child of God."

CLOSING
(up to 5 minutes)

OPTION 1: CHEATING SCARS

Give students each a piece of black construction paper, a pencil and an eraser. Have students each write the word "cheating" in big letters on their paper.

Say: **Many people who cheat believe cheating never hurts anyone. But cheating has lasting consequences.**

Have students each erase the word from their construction paper.

Ask:

- **What do you notice about the word on your paper?** (It's still there; I can still read it.)
- **How is this remaining image of the word "cheating" like what happens when you cheat?** (They both last beyond the actual event; they're different.)
- **What are some lasting consequences of cheating?** (Loss of respect by others; loss of self-respect; lack of true understanding of a subject; guilt.)

Say: **Just as Zacchaeus could change his ways, we can also overcome cheating habits.**

Form a circle. Close with prayer, asking God to help everyone overcome the temptation to cheat. Then, all at once, have teenagers each tear their black construction paper in half to symbolize beating the temptation.

OPTION 2: ANTI-CHEATERS CLUB

Have students quietly think about areas in their lives where they're tempted to cheat. Then say: **If you're tempted to cheat in school, you're not alone. But by encouraging each other, we can fight the temptation to cheat.**

Give students each a marker.

Have them go around to each of the posters made in the Students Against Cheating activity and sign them. Then form a circle and join hands. Have volunteers close with prayer, thanking God for the support of friends and asking him for strength to overcome the temptation to cheat.

If You Still Have Time . . .

Test Continuums—Set up a continuum in your room. Designate one end of the room as the "Lots" end and the other as the "None" end of the scale. Then have students stand somewhere between the two ends of the scale, based on how they'd answer the following questions:

- How much anxiety do you feel when you know a big test is coming?
- How much time do you spend studying for a big test?
- How much of an urge to cheat do you feel when you're facing an important test?
- How much should test grades affect your final grade for the class?
- How much cheating is there in your school?

Form a circle and discuss what teenagers learned from the activity.

Story Time—Form groups of no more than five. Have groups each create a children's story that teaches the consequences of cheating. Encourage teenagers to be creative in their stories. Then have them read or act out the stories for the rest of the groups. If possible, have teenagers read or act out their stories for a children's Sunday school class.

BIBLE POP QUIZ

Complete the following fill-in-the-blank questions.

1. Jeremiah's resolve to serve as one of God's prophets came after he complained he was ______________________.

2. David had ______________________'s husband killed in battle so David and she could be married.

3. The Old Testament prophet ______________________ tells of a four-faced creature with one face like a lion.

4. Paul and ______________________ were imprisoned in ______________________ when a miraculous earthquake broke their chains.

5. ______________________ was a prophet of God who was told to marry a prostitute. Her name was ______________________.

6. Besides the snake in the garden of Eden, ______________________'s donkey was the only other talking animal in the Bible.

7. ______________________ was born to Adam and Eve after the death of his brother, ______________________.

CASE STUDIES

CASE **#1**

The Pop Quiz Caper

Betsy always studies for her tests. She's an A-student. But when her biology teacher surprised the class with a pop quiz last week, Betsy couldn't remember the answer to one of the questions. Without thinking, she glanced over at Andre's paper for the answer. She was caught. What should her punishment be?

CASE **#2**

The History Horror

Juan is an average student. He knows each Friday he can expect a test in history. Usually he studies for the test, but this past week he had to take care of his little sister while his mom worked the evening shift. He knew he wouldn't remember all the dates and names for the test, so he wrote key answers on the palm of his hand Friday morning. He was caught. What should his punishment be?

CASE **#3**

The Algebra Final Frenzy

Sonia hates algebra. Sonia hates any math. No matter how hard she tries, she just doesn't understand it. But if she doesn't pass her Algebra 2 class, she won't graduate. So Sonia convinced her friend Tonya to sit next to her during the final exam. During the test, Sonia spent more time looking at Tonya's paper than her own. She was caught. What should her punishment be?

CASE **#4**

The Scholarship Snafu

Brian has a chance at a special combined athletic and academic scholarship to a well-respected university. As all-state quarterback, he's already met the athletic requirements. But he needs a good score on the university's special academic test. After hearing a rumor that test answers are available, Brian buys the answer sheet with money from his savings account and studies the answers. He's thrilled when the results from the test show his near-perfect score—until college officials contact him about a problem with the test. He was caught. What should Brian's punishment be?

LESSON 3

I DON'T HAVE TIME FOR HOMEWORK

Homework, homework, homework. Teachers give it. Parents nag about it. Students hate it.

Yet homework has always been around. There must be something worthwhile about homework.

LESSON AIM

To help teenagers recognize the value of studying.

OBJECTIVES

Students will:

- **discuss distractions to studying and homework;**
- **explore whose responsibility it is to learn;**
- **examine what the Bible says about developing individual talents and building foundations; and**
- **assess their study habits and attitudes.**

BIBLE BASIS

MATTHEW 7:24-27
MATTHEW 25:14-29

Look up the following scriptures. Then read the background paragraphs to see how the passages relate to your senior highers.

In **Matthew 7:24-27**, Jesus tells the parable of the wise and foolish builders.

In Palestine, a house-builder had to choose a site carefully. Many sandy spots turned into riverbeds when winter came. It took more work and energy to build on a stable rock foundation. But as the parable explains, the extra work paid off.

Teenagers are also in the building business. But they're building knowledge, not houses. And just like the foolish builder in the parable, many teenagers prefer the easy way out and would rather not spend much effort building their knowledge. Teenagers need to follow the example of the wise builder and dig through the sands of homework and studying to build a strong foundation for learning.

In **Matthew 25:14-29**, Jesus tells the parable of the talents.

Jesus' message: It doesn't matter how much we have, but what we do with what we have.

Each student has some academic talent. By applying the message of this parable, teenagers can understand it's important to do the best they can with their abilities. Students who invest their time and effort in learning are like the wise servants who invested their talents.

THIS LESSON AT A GLANCE

Section	Minutes	What Students Will Do	Supplies
Opener (Option 1)	5 to 10	**Distraction Attractions**—List distractions to studying or doing homework.	Radio, television, food, newsprint, markers, tape
(Option 2)		**Time's Up**—Experience how difficult it is to gauge time.	Watch with a second hand
Action and Reflection	10 to 15	**Homework Surprise**—Discover the value of studying.	Bag of candy
Bible Application	10 to 15	**Homework Parables**—Design a newspaper front page based on the messages in two parables.	Bibles, paper, magazines, tape, markers
Commitment	10 to 15	**How Well Do You Study?**—Discover how well they study.	"Study Habits Inventory" handouts (p. 32), pencils
Closing (Option 1)	up to 5	**A+ Attitudes**—Read a litany of good study attitudes.	"A+ Attitudes" handouts (p. 33)
(Option 2)		**One Subject at a Time**—Pray together for good study attitudes.	

The Lesson

OPENER

(5 to 10 minutes)

OPTION 1: DISTRACTION ATTRACTIONS

Turn on a radio and a television if possible. Place a variety of food items around the room. As kids enter the room, tell them they can eat the food during the opener.

Form groups of no more than six. Give each group a sheet

of newsprint and a marker. Have the groups brainstorm as many distractions to studying as possible in two minutes. Ask them to write the distractions on the newsprint.

After time is up, turn off the radio and television. Tape the distraction lists to the wall.

Ask:

● **Were you surprised at the number of distractions you listed? Why or why not?** (Yes, I didn't think there were so many; no, I know there are a lot; yes, I thought we'd list more.)

● **How easy was it for you to work with the radio and television on?**

● **If you had a choice between a room with loud music and a room that's completely quiet to study in, which would you choose? Explain.** (The loud room, I like the noise; the quiet room, I can't think around noise.)

● **What distraction on the list is hardest for you to ignore? Explain.**

Say: **Studying means different things to different people. What works for you may be a distraction to someone else. But regardless of the method you use, studying is important. Today we'll discover just how important.**

OPTION 2: TIME'S UP

Form pairs. Have partners stand facing each other. Say: **On "go," tell each other everything you did yesterday—from the time you woke up until you went to sleep. Both of you should talk at the same time. When you think you've talked for two minutes, sit down. You may not look at a watch or clock. You don't have to sit down when your partner does, but if you're standing, you still need to be talking. I'll call time when two minutes and five seconds are up. If you sit down more than five seconds before two minutes is up or you're still standing when I call time, you're out.**

After saying "go" make sure the students keep talking. Watch for students who sit down too early. When two minutes and five seconds are up, call time. Congratulate any students who sat down between five seconds before and five seconds after two minutes.

Then ask:

● **How easy was it to judge the time accurately?**

● **Did you feel any pressure to sit down? Why or why not?** (Yes, when everyone else started to sit down, I thought I might be wrong; yes, time seemed to go very slowly; no, I thought I judged the time well.)

● **How is this exercise like the way some people manage their time?** (They have more time than they think; they have less time than they think.)

● **If you sat down early, what did you do with the remaining few seconds?** (I just sat there; nothing; watched everyone else.)

● **If you added up all the time you did nothing during a day, how much time would you have?**

● **Do your days seem to go too fast or too slow? Explain.** (Too fast, I never have time to do things I want to do; too slow, school drags on forever.)

Say: **As we just demonstrated, judging time isn't always easy. But by learning to be efficient with our time, we can accomplish more. When it comes to studying, finding time is critical. Today, we'll see how important it is to find time for studying.**

ACTION AND REFLECTION

(10 to 15 minutes)

HOMEWORK SURPRISE

Form two groups. One group will be the study group and the other will be the didn't-study group. Say: **Imagine you were given homework assignments yesterday that apply to a test you'll be taking today.**

Take aside the members of the study group and say: **Your homework assignment simply said: "Each time I ask a question during the verbal test, *don't* answer. Even though I'll say the first person who stands and answers will get a prize, actually, the people who don't stand will get a prize. Remember, no matter what I say, *don't* answer."**

Gather both groups together. Say: **I hope you all read your homework assignment last night. Those of you who did will have a chance to win a piece of candy. Here are the five test questions. The first person who stands and answers will get a prize.**

Ask the following questions. Each time someone stands and answers one, have him or her stand near you in the front of the room. During the questions, encourage the kids who "studied" to "get with it" and answer the questions.

1. **Name a state that starts with the letter A.** (Alaska; Arkansas; Alabama; Arizona.)
2. **What is the sixth letter of the alphabet.** (F.)
3. **What three colors make up the American flag?** (Red, white and blue.)
4. **What's the square root of 81?** (Nine.)
5. **True or false? The second President of the United States was Abraham Lincoln.** (False.)

Tell students the quiz is over. Then give candy to the people who didn't answer any questions. Say: **If you'd read your homework assignment, you'd know you weren't supposed to answer any questions today.**

Ask the didn't-study group:

● **How did you feel when you didn't get a piece of candy?** (Angry; cheated; embarrassed.)

● **How important was it to complete the homework assignment?** (Very important; somewhat important; not important.)

Distribute a piece of candy to those teenagers who didn't get one. Then ask:

● **Whose responsibility is learning? Explain.** (The students', they're the ones who can choose to listen or not; the teachers', they're paid to teach.)

● **What's the value of studying or doing homework?** (You'll learn more; there's no value; it helps you get better grades.)

Say: **By studying or doing your homework, you'll know what teachers expect from you. Plus, you'll learn more and develop good habits for when you're in college or working. Better grades are the result of studying, but better habits and increased learning are the goals.**

BIBLE APPLICATION

(10 to 15 minutes)

HOMEWORK PARABLES

Form groups of no more than five. Assign each group one of the following scriptures: Matthew 7:24-27 or Matthew 25:14-29. Have groups each read and discuss their scripture. Then give each group a supply of heavy paper, magazines, tape and markers. Have teenagers design the front page of a newspaper with a feature story depicting the scripture message as it relates to homework.

Ask:

● **How can this scripture apply to homework?** (For Matthew 7:24-27: Learning isn't easy; it's important to build a solid foundation of knowledge; the consequences of doing things the lazy way can be bad. For Matthew 25:14-29: Doing your homework is like investing the talents; you only get what you put into your schoolwork.)

● **How is this verse applicable to your life?** (I need to study more; I need to invest my time more wisely; it isn't.)

COMMITMENT

(10 to 15 minutes)

HOW WELL DO YOU STUDY?

Say: **Homework doesn't come easily to everyone. Some of us are organized; some of us don't know what a notebook divider is. What's your homework efficiency quota? What are your strengths? weaknesses?**

Distribute a copy of the "Study Habits Inventory" (p. 32) and a pencil to each student. Ask teenagers to complete the inventory and score it according to the instructions. Explain that they won't have to share all their answers, but encourage them to discuss their top study strength. Form groups of no more than four. Ask kids to share their study strengths.

Form pairs. Have partners each choose one study weakness to work on during the coming week. Then have partners make a verbal commitment to each other to work on that study weakness. Have teenagers each describe one positive quality they see in their partner that can help him or her stick to the commitment. Encourage partners to check up on one another during the week.

OPTION 1: A+ ATTITUDES

Have students stay with their partners from How Well Do You Study? Have them sit facing each other. Give an "A+ Attitudes" sheet (p. 33) to each student. Ask one partner to be "A" and the other to be "B." Then, have students read their parts of the reading in unison, filling in the name of their partner where applicable.

OPTION 2: ONE SUBJECT AT A TIME

Have the group stand in a circle, holding hands. Say: **Since we study one subject at a time, we'll close with a one-word-at-a-time prayer.**

Explain that you'll begin a prayer with one word and then each person—moving clockwise around the circle—will add one word to yours to build it into a sentence prayer. Depending on the size of your class, you might go around the circle a few times and have more than one sentence in the prayer. Determine beforehand how many times you'll go around the circle so teenagers know when to end the prayer.

CLOSING

(up to 5 minutes)

If You Still Have Time . . .

Homework Blues Song—Form groups of no more than five. Have groups each write a sad song about homework to the tune of "Row, Row, Row Your Boat" or another familiar tune. Have them perform the songs for each other. Then discuss why people don't like homework.

Study Positions—Call out subjects that teenagers study. Have them get into a position that describes how studying for that subject makes them feel. For example, someone who hates studying for math might hide under a table or curl up in a fetal position. Include subjects such as: English, math, science, physical education, music, geography, history, literature and art. Then discuss which subjects are the easiest and most difficult to study.

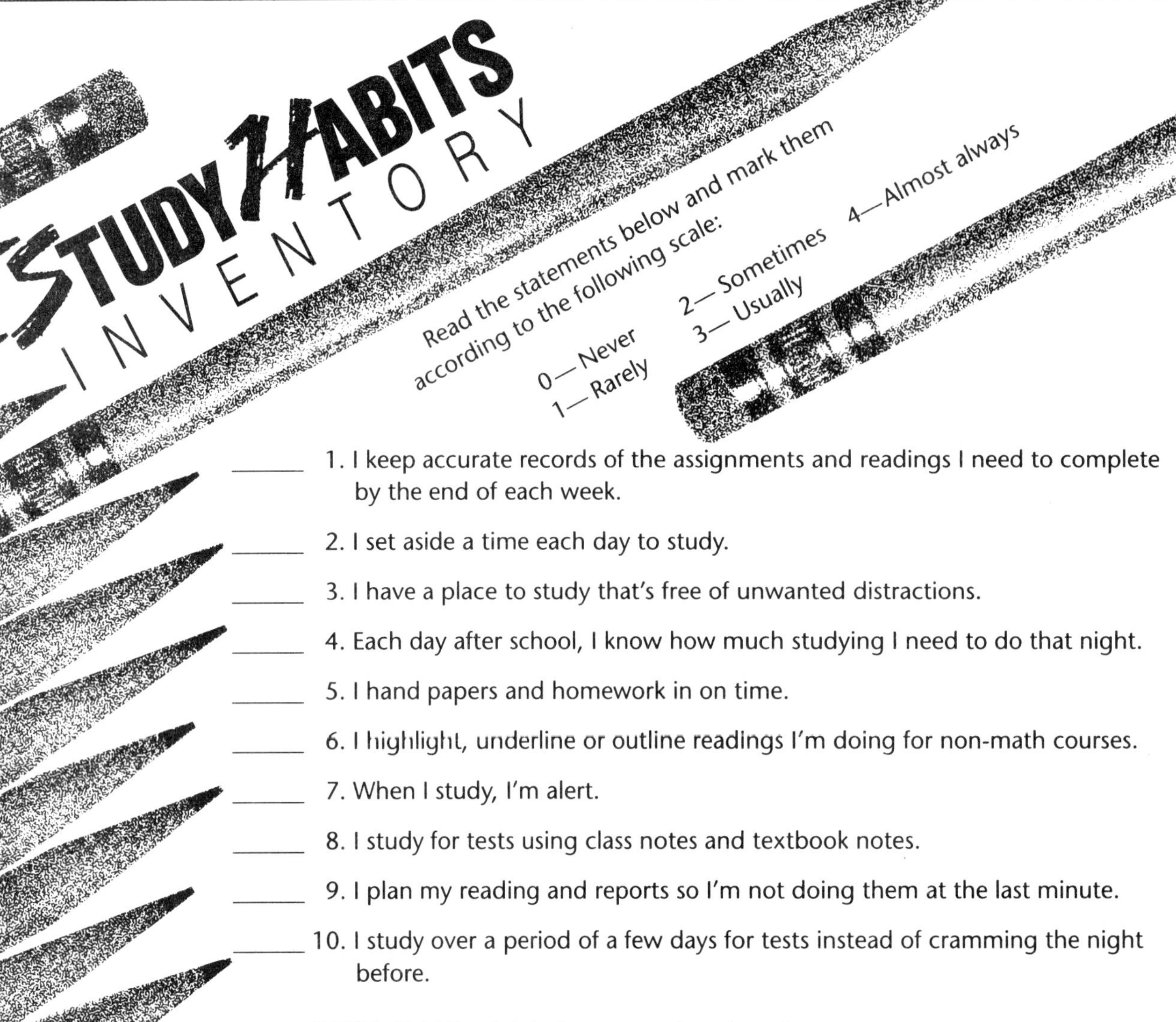

_____ 1. I keep accurate records of the assignments and readings I need to complete by the end of each week.

_____ 2. I set aside a time each day to study.

_____ 3. I have a place to study that's free of unwanted distractions.

_____ 4. Each day after school, I know how much studying I need to do that night.

_____ 5. I hand papers and homework in on time.

_____ 6. I highlight, underline or outline readings I'm doing for non-math courses.

_____ 7. When I study, I'm alert.

_____ 8. I study for tests using class notes and textbook notes.

_____ 9. I plan my reading and reports so I'm not doing them at the last minute.

_____ 10. I study over a period of a few days for tests instead of cramming the night before.

_____ TOTAL (Add the total of your numbers here.)

Look at your total score. Then check out where you fit in the following scale.

Points	**Evaluation**
35 to 40	You exhibit excellent study habits. You're likely getting the best possible grades you can.
28 to 34	You show solid study habits, but you can improve them and possibly improve your grades.
20 to 27	You're getting by. But with better discipline you could improve your grades. Find your lowest scores and work on those areas.
0 to 20	You have lots of room for improvement. Read the suggestions on this inventory and talk with a parent or teacher to see how you can put these ideas into practice.

A: (name), have a positive attitude about school.

B: And (name), don't look down at homework or studying.

A: Refuse to believe that grades are perfect measures,

B: But understand that doing your best is important.

A: God, help us to develop good school study habits,

B: By making lists and following through;

A: By refusing to put off things that can be done today;

B: By asking for help when we need it;

A: And by developing an inner motivation to stretch our abilities.

B: Teach us discipline,

A: To replace our cries for last-minute miracles.

B: And help us develop good spiritual study habits,

A: So our faith may grow.

Both A and B: **Help us to be the best we can be, striving to do our best in school as an example of our striving to know you better.**

LESSON 4

SO MUCH TO DO . . .

The competition for a high schooler's time is fierce. Academics, athletics, music lessons, part-time jobs, church activities and dating all demand attention. So many choices and so little time can overwhelm a high school student with the pressures of having too much to do. Decision-making becomes a critical part of high school life.

LESSON AIM

To help teenagers manage their time, balancing activities and academics.

OBJECTIVES

Students will:

- **identify activities they're currently involved in;**
- **examine their priorities;**
- **explore what the Bible says about stress and overload; and**
- **assess their goals using a small-step-at-a-time management system.**

BIBLE BASIS

ECCLESIASTES 3:1-8
LUKE 10:38-42

Look up the following scriptures. Then read the background paragraphs to see how the passages relate to your senior highers.

Ecclesiastes 3:1-8 states there's a time for everything under heaven.

In this passage, the writer ponders God's design for life. He describes the times of life as if they were all divinely appointed. This passage examines God's timing of life's events.

God's timing and our timing are often different. Teenagers sometimes feel there isn't enough time to do the things they want to do. They try to fit more things than possible into their busy days. Following the advice of this passage, teenagers can learn that God's timing may not always be the same as their timing. There's a time for everything, but that time isn't always when we think it is.

In **Luke 10:38-42**, Jesus visits Martha and Mary. Martha's preoccupation with elaborate preparations for the meal took precedence over spending time with Jesus. So Jesus wanted her to re-examine her priorities.

Teenagers have many demands on their time. And Jesus' advice to Martha is just as valid for teenagers. When they get caught up in worries and stresses of mega-activities, teenagers need to slow down and prioritize their time.

THIS LESSON AT A GLANCE

Section	Minutes	What Students Will Do	Supplies
Opener (Option 1)	5 to 10	**All Tied Up**—Experience how it feels to be tied up by many different activities.	Ropes or string
(Option 2)		**Pressure Cooker**—Bombard a volunteer with deadlines.	"Pressure Cooker" handouts (p. 40)
Action and Reflection	10 to 15	**Sands of Time**—Experience how it feels to organize an out-of-control schedule.	Newsprint, marker, paper, sand, Bibles
Bible Application	10 to 15	**Worry, Worry, Worry**—Pantomime and discuss priorities and worrying.	Bibles
Commitment	5 to 10	**Baby Steps**—Decide on steps to reach a goal.	"Baby Steps" handout (p. 41), pencils, hourglass or egg timer
Closing (Option 1)	5 to 10	**Diploma Pass**—Pass papers quickly around a circle.	Paper, string, pencils
(Option 2)		**Hourglass Prayer**—Pray together silently.	Hourglass or egg timer

The Lesson

OPENER
(5 to 10 minutes)

OPTION 1: ALL TIED UP

Form two teams. Give each team a 20-foot length of rope or string. Have kids stretch out the ropes along the floor. Use a hallway if necessary. Have team members line up along their rope, spacing themselves evenly from one end to the other. Designate a starting end for each rope.

Say: **On "go," pick up the rope and begin to tie single**

knots in it. The person standing closest to the starting end will tie the first knot. Then in succession, each person will tie a knot near the spot where he or she is holding the rope. Team members will have to release their hold on the rope as subsequent knots are tied. But before another knot can be tied, the team members must all grab the rope and pull it taut. As a knot is tied, the person tying it must call out a school activity he or she is involved in. The first team to get all the knots tied will win. Ready, set, go!

Declare the winner.

Ask:

- **How are the knots tied in the rope like the way you feel when you get involved in too many activities or don't manage your time well?** (It's like I have knots in my stomach; I feel stressed out; uneven, that's how I feel when I'm too busy.)

Say: **It's easy to get so busy you don't have time for everything you want or need to do. Today, we'll look at ways you can manage your time so that doesn't happen.**

OPTION 2: PRESSURE COOKER

Form a circle. Have a volunteer stand in the center of the circle. Distribute copies of the "Pressure Cooker" handouts (p. 40). On "go," have the teenagers in the circle call out the statements on the list and others they come up with. Encourage them to call out statements with a sense of urgency and necessity. After a minute of bombarding the volunteer with deadlines and tasks, call time.

Ask the volunteer:

- **How did it feel to have everyone remind you of your obligations?** (Anxious; confused; it didn't bother me.)
- **Can you remember all the deadlines and tasks people called out? Why or why not?** (No, there were too many; no, everyone was talking at once.)

Ask everyone:

- **How is this like real life?** (I've got too many demands on my time; it isn't; I can't remember all the things I've got to do.)

Say: **Today, we're going to examine ways to keep from getting so busy that we feel like the volunteer in this activity.**

BIBLE APPLICATION
(10 to 15 minutes)

SANDS OF TIME

Have teenagers tell all the activities they're involved with—in and out of school—and how much time they spend on each during the week. List these on a sheet of newsprint.

Have teenagers sit around a table. Place a piece of paper in front of each student. Then go around and pour a small amount of sand onto each piece of paper. Say: **Imagine each**

grain of sand is an activity in your life. When we don't prioritize our schedules, it's like the sand is just dropped on us.

Ask:

- **Look at the list on the newsprint. How is this list like the grains of sand on the paper?** (There are a lot of activities; it's a jumbled mess.)
- **How do you feel when you've got too much to do and too little time?** (Frustrated; angry; confused.)

Say: **When we learn to set priorities, our schedule begins to take on a recognizable shape.**

As you speak, show teenagers how to carefully roll up the paper with the sand on it and make it into a funnel. Be sure one end of the funnel is very small. Then begin drawing a geometric shape by letting the sand flow slowly onto the table. Encourage teenagers to do the same. Say: **Just as we can learn to take the jumble of sand and organize it, we can learn to prioritize and organize our busy schedules.**

Have someone read Ecclesiastes 3:1-8.

Ask:

- **Is there really a time for everything? Explain.** (Yes, but we don't use our time wisely; no, there's too much going on.)

BIBLE APPLICATION
(10 to 15 minutes)

WORRY, WORRY, WORRY

Say: **Many people have busy schedules—juggling school, friends, sports and other activities. But while some are just hoping to make it through the week, others seem to move from one activity to the next without much stress at all.**

Have someone read aloud Luke 10:38-42. Have three volunteers act out the story as it's read. Encourage them to exaggerate Mary's quiet nature and Martha's frantic personality.

Ask which person—Mary or Martha—the students most relate to. Have "Marthas" run around frantically and "Marys" sit quietly. Form two groups based on their responses. Then have the groups answer the following questions:

- **In what specific ways are you like Mary or Martha?** (I rush around a lot like Martha; I'm usually calm like Mary.)
- **What kinds of worries do you have?** (School; homework; family problems; friends; work.)
- **Rate your stress level from 1 to 10 (1=a calm rating; 10=a rating on the Richter scale).**
- **What are the advantages of having a Mary- or Martha-type personality?** (If you're like Martha, you might get more done in life; if you're like Mary, you can handle stress better.)
- **What are the disadvantages?** (Martha-types get too stressed out; Mary-types might get lazy.)

Form a circle.

Ask:

• **What was Martha's top priority in this scripture?** (Preparing for the meal.)

• **What was Mary's top priority?** (Talking with Jesus.)

• **How do you set priorities?** (I don't; I base them on what has to be done; I do what I want to first.)

Say: **Mary and Martha had different reactions to the situation as recorded in Luke. Whether we're more like Mary or Martha, we still need to learn how to manage our school and non-school activities.**

COMMITMENT

(5 to 10 minutes)

BABY STEPS

Distribute the "Baby Steps" handout (p. 41) and pencils. Have students complete the Top 10 Priorities section of the handout. Then form pairs, and have partners briefly discuss their lists. Say: **It's not always easy to follow the priorities we set. But by setting a goal and then taking small steps toward that goal, we can begin to make our school and non-school activities fit into our priority list where they should.**

Have teenagers each determine one academic and one non-academic goal based on their Top 10 Priorities list. Have them list these in the two big feet on the handout. Then have partners work together to determine five "baby steps" they each can take to reach their goals. Explain that each baby step must be reachable in no more than one week's time. Refer to the "Baby Steps Sample" box for an idea on how to complete the handout.

Place an hourglass or egg timer in the center of the room. Flip it so the sand starts to fall. Then say: **As the sand falls a few grains at a time, so we need to pursue our school and non-school goals in small steps—little by little. Before the sand runs out, make a silent commitment to taking steps toward your goals.**

Baby Steps Sample

Big Foot Goal	To raise my English grade from a C to an A.
Baby Step #1	Spend one hour a day studying English.
Baby Step #2	Ask at least one question each day in class.
Baby Step #3	Find out about extra-credit ideas and do some.
Baby Step #4	Study for tests with a friend.
Baby Step #5	Hand papers in on time.

Table Talk

The Table Talk activity in this course helps teenagers and parents talk about school-related issues.

If you choose to use the Table Talk activity here, this is a good time to show students the "Table Talk" handout (p. 42). Ask them to spend time with their parents completing it. Before kids leave, give them each the "Table Talk" handout to take home, or tell them you'll send it to their parents.

Or use the Table Talk idea found in the Bonus Ideas (p. 44) for a meeting based on the handout.

CLOSING

(5 to 10 minutes)

OPTION 1: DIPLOMA PASS

Give students each three pieces of paper and three 6-inch lengths of string. Form three groups. Have teenagers in one group list on their papers school-related demands on their time. Have teenagers in another group list non-school demands on their time and attention. Have the third group list essential daily activities that take time, such as sleeping, eating and bathing. Then have teenagers each roll up their papers and tie the strings around them to make the papers look like diplomas.

Form a circle. Say: **Learning to balance all the school, non-school and essential activities each day isn't easy. On "go," begin passing the diplomas clockwise around the circle as fast as you can. If someone drops one, he or she is out and must leave the circle—but his or her diplomas stay in the circle.**

Say: **Go.**

After a few diplomas have been dropped or things get out of hand, stop the game and place the diplomas in the center of the circle. Say: **Sometimes we feel we're trying to hold on to too many things. But with each other's help and God's guidance, we can balance all of our activities.**

Thank each teenager for his or her contributions to the course. Say: **"(Name), I've really appreciated you in this class because ..."**

Close with prayer.

OPTION 2: HOURGLASS PRAYER

Say: **One of our top priorities can be to spend time with God. As we learn to balance our school time with other activities, let's seek God's guidance.**

Thank each teenager for his or her contributions to the course. Say: **"(Name), I've really appreciated you in this class because ..."**

Flip the hourglass or egg timer and have teenagers spend the time in silent prayer. If the hourglass or egg timer lasts one minute or less, flip it more than once so kids have about three minutes for silent prayer.

If You Still Have Time ...

Priority Realities—Have the students look at their Top 10 Priorities on the "Baby Steps" handout. Then have them think back on a recent week and see how their activities match up with their priority lists. Ask teenagers if reality matched the priority list. Then discuss why it did or didn't and how to better match reality with the desired priorities.

A Slice of Life—Give kids each a paper plate. Have them each cut the plate into slices that represent various activities they participate in each week. Form pairs to discuss which slices were the largest and smallest and why.

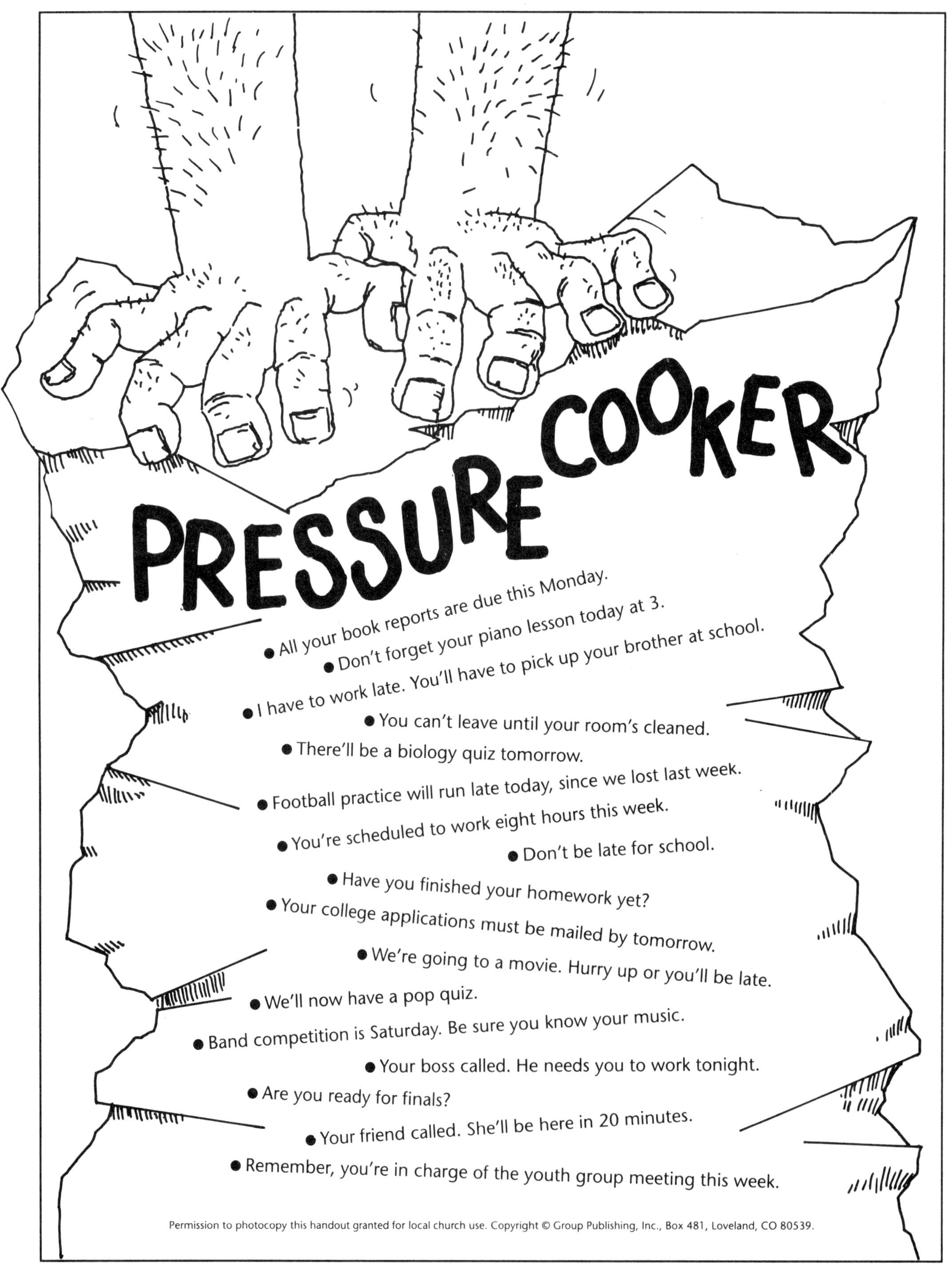
PRESSURE COOKER
• All your book reports are due this Monday.
• Don't forget your piano lesson today at 3.
• I have to work late. You'll have to pick up your brother at school.
• You can't leave until your room's cleaned.
• There'll be a biology quiz tomorrow.
• Football practice will run late today, since we lost last week.
• You're scheduled to work eight hours this week.
• Don't be late for school.
• Have you finished your homework yet?
• Your college applications must be mailed by tomorrow.
• We're going to a movie. Hurry up or you'll be late.
• We'll now have a pop quiz.
• Band competition is Saturday. Be sure you know your music.
• Your boss called. He needs you to work tonight.
• Are you ready for finals?
• Your friend called. She'll be here in 20 minutes.
• Remember, you're in charge of the youth group meeting this week.

Baby Steps

Top 10 Priorities

What are your top 10 priorities in life? Include school and other activities and rank them in the following spaces.

1. ____________________
2. ____________________
3. ____________________
4. ____________________
5. ____________________
6. ____________________
7. ____________________
8 ____________________
9. ____________________
10. ____________________

Baby Step #1

Baby Step #2

Baby Step #3

Baby Step #4

Baby Step #5

Big Foot Goal

Baby Step #1

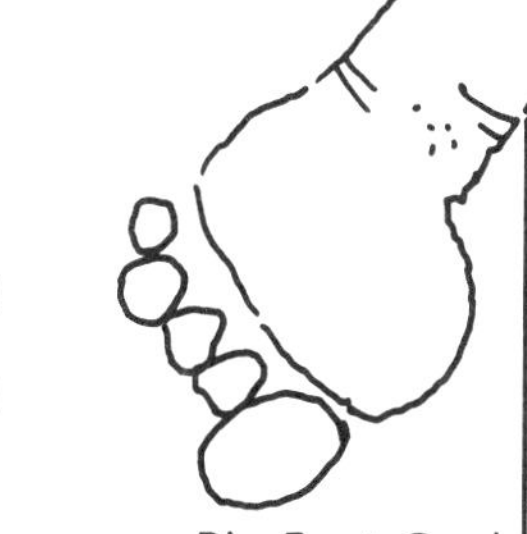

Big Foot Goal

Baby Step #5

Baby Step #4

Baby Step #3

Baby Step #2

Table Talk

To the parent: We're talking about school struggles at church. Please take a few minutes to sit down with your teenager and talk about school stress. Use this sheet to spark discussion about the topic.

Teenager

Answer the following questions or complete the statements based on this year in high school.

Parent

Answer the following questions or complete the statements based on your high school years. Then answer the success questions again as they apply to your current situation.

School Subjects
- What's your favorite subject in school? Why?
- What's your least favorite subject? Why?
- The easiest subject for me is ...
- The subject I struggle with most is ...

Grades and Report Cards
- How important are grades? Explain.
- Grades are stressful because ...
- Grades should be ...
- A time I felt good about a grade I received was ...
- A time I felt bad about a grade I received was ...

Success
- What is success?
- What role does school play in a person's ability to succeed?
- School successes I've had include ...

Extracurricular Activities
- The activities that interest me most include ...
- The activities I'm involved in now include ...
- Extracurricular activities are important because ...
- What are negative aspects of extracurricular activities?

Cheating
- I believe cheating is ...
- A time I cheated and regretted it was ...

Parent

Get out your high school or college yearbook and look through it with your teenager. Share your memories and talk about how they relate to today's situation.

Teenager

Show your parent some of your school books. Talk about the subjects that are easy for you and the ones that aren't.

Parent and teenager

Read the following scripture together. Then give at least two reasons why you think your parent or teenager is successful according to this scripture.

"Brothers, I do not consider myself yet to have taken hold of it. But one thing I do: Forgetting what is behind and straining toward what is ahead, I press on toward the goal to win the prize for which God called me heavenward in Christ Jesus" (Philippians 3:13-14).

BONUS IDEAS

MEETINGS AND MORE

Homework Happening—Plan a monthly homework gathering. Invite adults from your church and local teachers to come help students with homework questions. Set up a "quiet room" for students who study best in that environment. Also set up a "busy room" where music and talking are permitted. Provide plenty of beverages and snacks. Show students that homework can be fun.

Popular Professor Panel—Take a survey of kids' favorite teachers. Then invite those teachers to participate in a panel discussion. Have teenagers prepare questions ahead of time. Include such questions as: What made you decide to become a teacher? What's the best part of teaching? the worst? Why is school important?

Dunce Cap Burning—On a piece of construction paper, have kids list times they felt inadequate because of school, grades or activity pressures. Have kids each create a construction paper dunce cap from their list. Start a small fire in a metal garbage can. Then have kids burn the dunce caps as a symbol of God's ability to reach beyond their feelings of inadequacy. Read aloud 1 John 3:1 and affirm God's love for each person.

Lunch Break—If possible, arrange to meet your students in their territory—the school cafeteria. If schools in your area won't allow you on campus, take teenagers to their favorite off-campus lunch spot. Talk with them about their day at school. Find out what's going well and what's not.

School Survey—Have kids develop a survey on school life. Include these questions: How many hours a day do you spend on homework? What's your favorite subject? your least favorite? What makes a good teacher? a poor teacher? What's the best thing about school? the worst?

Have kids get permission to distribute the survey at school. Then help them compile and discuss the results. Your school board officials might also be interested in what you discover.

Yearbook Exchange—Invite the congregation to a Yearbook Exchange Extravaganza. Have congregation members and students each bring a "school lunch" and any old high school yearbooks they can find. After lunch, form groups that include both old and young people, and have them share high school memories and experiences. Have groups discuss the differences between school then and now.

Table Talk—Use the "Table Talk" handout (p. 42) as the basis for a parents and teenagers' meeting. Distribute the handout before the meeting. Have parents bring their high school yearbooks, photos and other memorabilia to the meeting. Open the meeting with a fun skit where parents and teenagers switch roles.

The Three R's (Really, Really Ridiculous)—Give teenagers each a pencil and a copy of "The Three R's (Really, Really Ridiculous)" handout (p. 46). Have them follow the instructions and complete it. If you have a small class, allow teenagers each to complete more than two subjects. Afterward, talk about the value of the various subjects taught in high school.

PARTY PLEASERS

Freshmen Prep Party—Before a new school year begins, plan a party for the incoming freshmen. Have upperclassmen share "freshman" success stories. Have the incoming freshmen write anonymous questions for the upperclassmen to answer about high school life. Serve "fresh" food such as crisp salads or fresh fruit. Play "academic" games such as Monopoly, Chess, Scrabble or Trivial Pursuit.

Senior Salute—"Roast" the seniors in your class. Have non-seniors collect pictures and interesting school facts about each senior. Invite all the students to a meal. Roast hot dogs, corn and marshmallows over a fire. After dinner, have non-seniors present the facts and pictures about each senior in a "This is Your Life" format. End the party with a more serious affirmation time for the seniors.

RETREAT AND LOCK-IN IDEAS

School "Daze" Retreat—Plan a retreat—following midterms or finals—that will allow kids to unwind from school pressures. Include wild and crazy activities such as relay races and scavenger hunts. Allow plenty of time for the three R's—resting, relaxing and recovering. Serve "fried brain" foods such as homemade french fries, fried chicken and fried eggs. Do a Bible study for "study hall." Plan a food fight with whipped cream pies and marshmallows—outside the eating area for easy cleanup. Close the retreat with a homework assignment—everyone has to spend one hour alone in silent time with God.

Intergroup Lock-In—Plan a lock-in with several different churches. Form groups that mix and match the kids with members of other groups. Have groups each do crowdbreakers, crazy games and fun skits to help build community. For crowdbreaker and community-building ideas, check out *Quick Crowdbreakers and Games for Youth Groups* (Group Books) and *Building Community in Youth Groups* (Group Books). Then have students go to different "classrooms" to discuss various aspects of school, such as tests, teachers, after-school activities and grades. Every hour or so, have kids change classes. Include fun times for games and skits between each "class period." Plan for at least a few hours of sleep.

After breakfast, have groups each present a portion of a worship service. During the worship, have kids use fabric paint to create T-shirts celebrating something they learned during the lock-in.

Encourage kids to wear their new shirts to school on Monday.

THE THREE R'S (REALLY, REALLY RIDICULOUS)

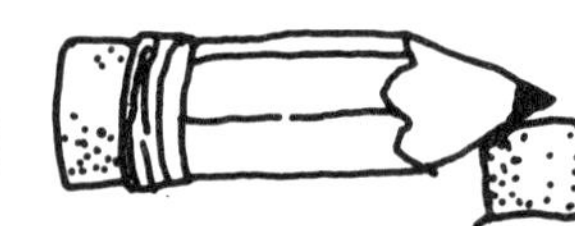

Be the first to graduate! Find people who'll complete each of the tasks below and sign their names. No more than two subjects may be completed on this sheet by any one person. To win, be the first person to have all the boxes completed.

Physical Education Do 10 sit-ups __________	**Speech** Recite aloud, "Peter Piper picked a peck of pickled peppers" three times—fast! __________	**English** Write a 10-word essay on the meaning of life on the back of this sheet. __________
Geography Be a globe. Put your finger at the top of your head and spin five times. __________	**Yearbook** Strike a pose you wouldn't want seen in your yearbook.  __________	**Biology** Point to the following body parts: head, nose, eyes, ears, kneecap, foot, toes, ankle. __________
Math Multiply your age by seven. Write the answer here ________. __________	**Physics** Prove Newton's law of gravitation. Stand on a chair—then step off it. __________	**Language** Say hello in at least one language different from your native language. __________
Spelling Recite the alphabet backward (beginning with Z and ending with A). __________	**Reading** Find a Bible and read John 15:12 aloud.  __________	**History** Draw an outline of your country on the back of this paper and mark where you were born. __________

More from Group's Active Bible Curriculum

Yes, I want scripture-based learning that blasts away boredom.

For Senior High

Quantity

_______ 202-1 **Getting Along With Parents**
Help senior highers build quality relationships with their parents
ISBN 1-55945-202-1 $6.95

_______ 200-5 **Hazardous to Your Health**
Train senior high students to understand and avoid abusive lifestyles
ISBN 1-55945-200-5 $6.95

_______ 203-X **Is Marriage In Your Future?**
Help teenagers learn what they need to know now—so they can have a successful marriage and family life later
ISBN 1-55945-203-X $6.95

_______ 205-6 **Knowing God's Will**
Help teenagers discover God's will for their lives
ISBN 1-55945-205-6 $6.95

_______ 201-3 **School Struggles**
Train teenagers to turn school stress into school success
ISBN 1-55945-201-3 $6.95

_______ 204-8 **Your Life as a Disciple**
Help Christian teenagers develop a desire to serve God
ISBN 1-55945-204-8 $6.95

For Junior High/Middle School

Quantity

_______ 100-9 **Boosting Self-Esteem**
Help kids develop a positive self-image
ISBN 1-55945-100-9 $6.95

_______ 102-5 **Evil and the Occult**
Train junior highers to protect themselves against the trap of Satanism
ISBN 1-55945-102-5 $6.95

_______ 103-3 **Peer Pressure**
Teach students to make good decisions while keeping their friends
ISBN 1-55945-103-3 $6.95

_______ 104-1 **Prayer**
Help young people discover God through prayer
ISBN 1-55945-104-1 $6.95

_______ 101-7 **Today's Music: Good or Bad?**
Help teenagers make good decisions about music
ISBN 1-55945-101-7 $6.95

_______ 105-X **What's A Christian?**
Teach Christian teenagers the basics of their faith
ISBN 1-55945-105-X $6.95

Yes, please send me _______ of Group's Active Bible Curriculum™ studies at $6.95 each plus $3 postage and handling per order. Colorado residents add 3% sales tax.

03151

☐ Check enclosed ☐ VISA ☐ MasterCard
Credit card # ______________________
Good until ______________________

(Please print)
Name ______________________
Address ______________________
City ______________________ State ____________ ZIP ____________
Daytime phone (____) ______________________

Take this order form or a photocopy to your favorite Christian bookstore. Or mail to:

Group Books Active Bible Curriculum
Box 481 ● Loveland, CO 80539 ● (303) 669-3836